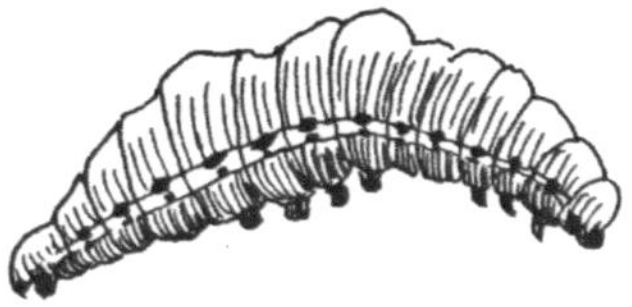

# THE CATERPILLAR AND THE BUTTERFLY

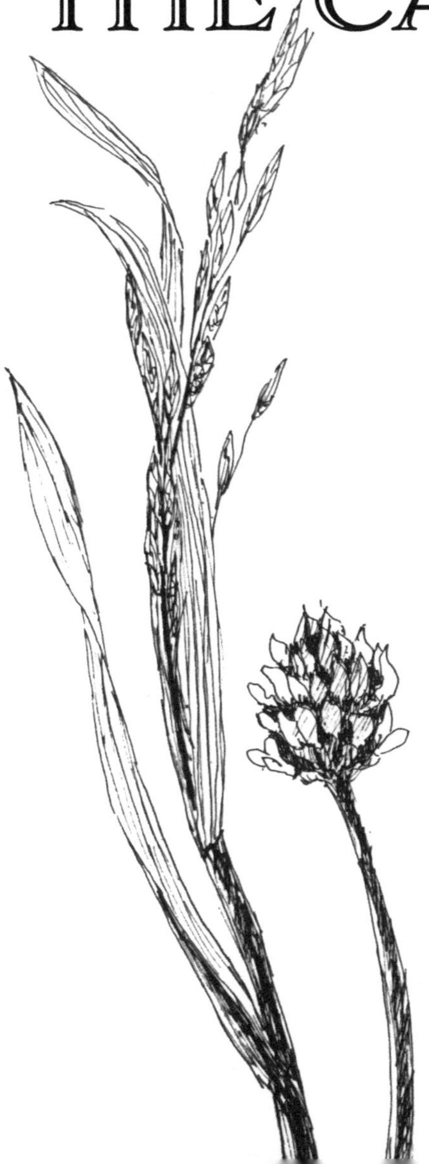

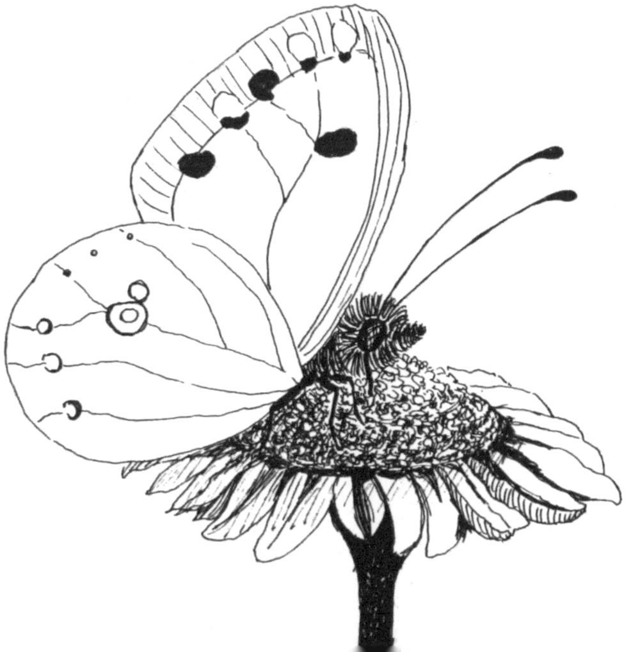

Ruth Lieberherr

*To my children: Andrea and Eva*
*And to my grandchildren: Tyler, Anna, Ella and Eida*

All rights reserved.
ISBN: 978-1-7328877-4-9

Text and Illustrations © 1985 Ruth Lieberherr
First Printed 1985 in Switzerland

New Edition 2019
Text and Illustrations © Ruth Lieberherr
Book Layout & Design by Carolyn Vaughan (CVaughanDesigns.com)

Printed in the United States.

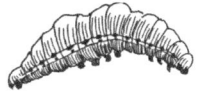

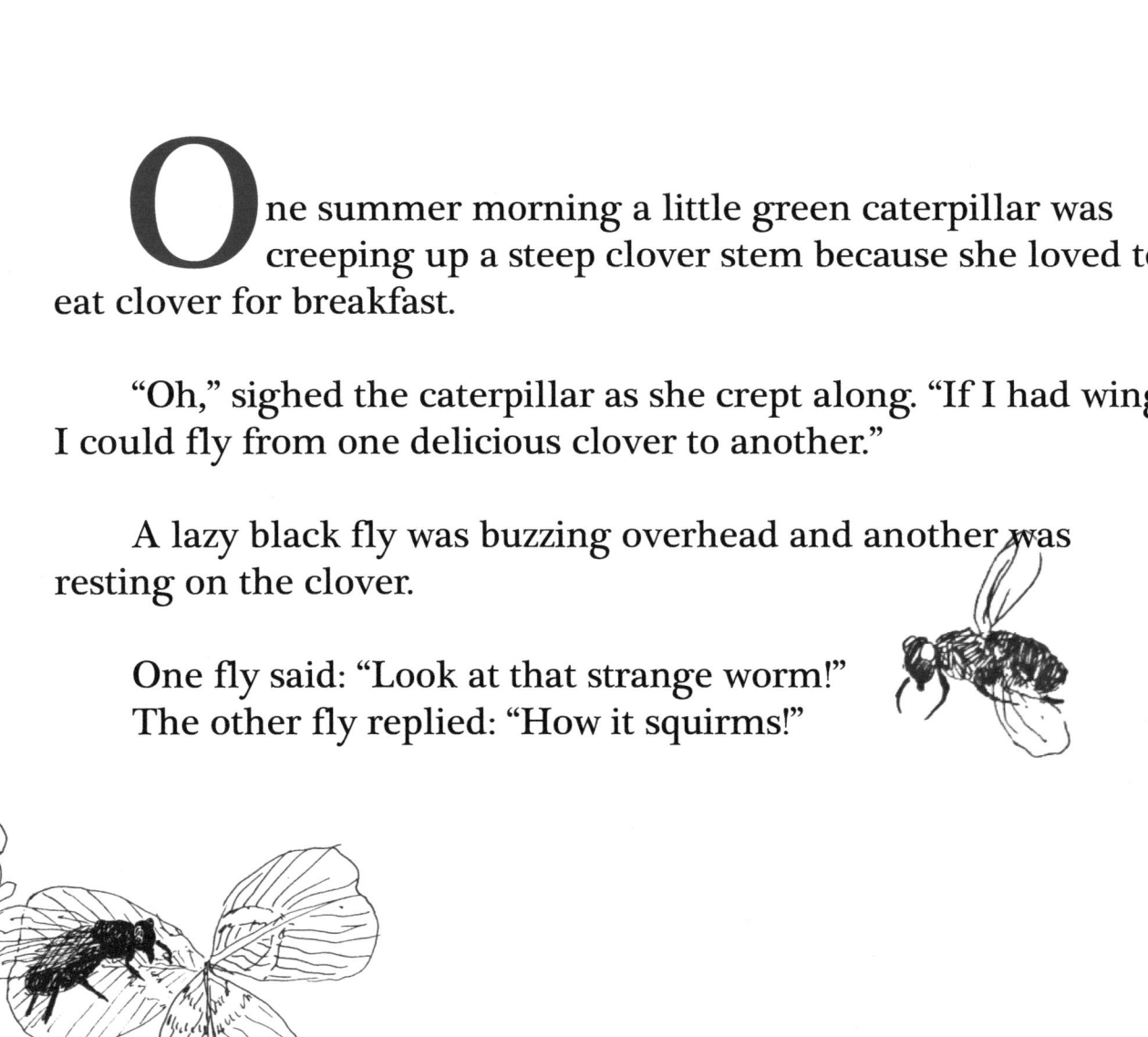

One summer morning a little green caterpillar was creeping up a steep clover stem because she loved to eat clover for breakfast.

"Oh," sighed the caterpillar as she crept along. "If I had wings, I could fly from one delicious clover to another."

A lazy black fly was buzzing overhead and another was resting on the clover.

One fly said: "Look at that strange worm!"
The other fly replied: "How it squirms!"

The caterpillar saw a big grasshopper on a blade of grass above her.

"If only I could jump like the grasshopper!" she said.

The grasshopper disappeared with a big proud jump.

Then she heard a kind voice. It was a little red ladybug sitting on a leaf.

The caterpillar said: "It is easy for you to be kind because you have wings!"

T he little caterpillar left the kind ladybug behind and ate a large breakfast.

Soon she met a gloomy old snail.

"Oh my, life is tiring for creatures like us," said the snail. "We have to crawl along so slowly."

"Why don't you leave your house at home?" the caterpillar asked.

"Leave my house at home?" the snail exclaimed indignantly. "It might rain."

The caterpillar thought to herself: "If I had a house, I could curl up and sleep. I feel tired."

So the caterpillar spun herself into a deep blanket and fell fast asleep.

Along came the ladybug again. "Where is the caterpillar?"

The gloomy snail replied: "Something terrible has probably happened to her."

The caterpillar, asleep in her chrysalis blanket, safely was dreaming of wings.

And one fine day the skin of the chrysalis burst open.
Out came a beautiful butterfly.

"How changed I feel," said the caterpillar. "Am I still dreaming?"

Along came the grasshopper hopping through the grass.

"Beautiful butterfly," he said. "Would you like to have a drop of dew or would you prefer some nectar?"

"Does he mean me?" the caterpillar asked herself.

The curious flies buzzed: " How beautiful you are."

The caterpillar cried out: "A miracle has happened to me! I have become a butterfly!"

And she flew happily through the shining air.

Soon she came upon the snail creeping sadly along. She wanted to share her joy with him.

"Maybe a similar miracle can happen to you," she said.

The snail would not believe that the beautiful butterfly once had been the little green caterpillar.

The snail warned: "You had better be careful. You may fall and hurt yourself."

The butterfly would not listen to the gloomy warnings of the snail. She flew into the clear blue sky towards the sun, which was shining very brightly.

"Look! What is that marvellous creature flying towards me?"

"I have seen lazy black flies, a big green grasshopper, a little red ladybug, and a gloomy old snail," she said. "But I have never seen as beautiful a creature as you are."

"Will you come and play with me?" sang the other butterfly.

"Oh yes," she replied.

A ll day long the two butterflies played hide-and-seek and tag among the beautiful flowers.

When they got tired, or hungry and thirsty, they rested on a flower and drank sweet nectar.

As the sun began to set, they found two comfortable flowers and fell asleep quite close together.

"Good night, sleep well," they said to each other.

And before it was quite dark they were dreaming of another day, when they would play together, again, among the beautiful flowers.

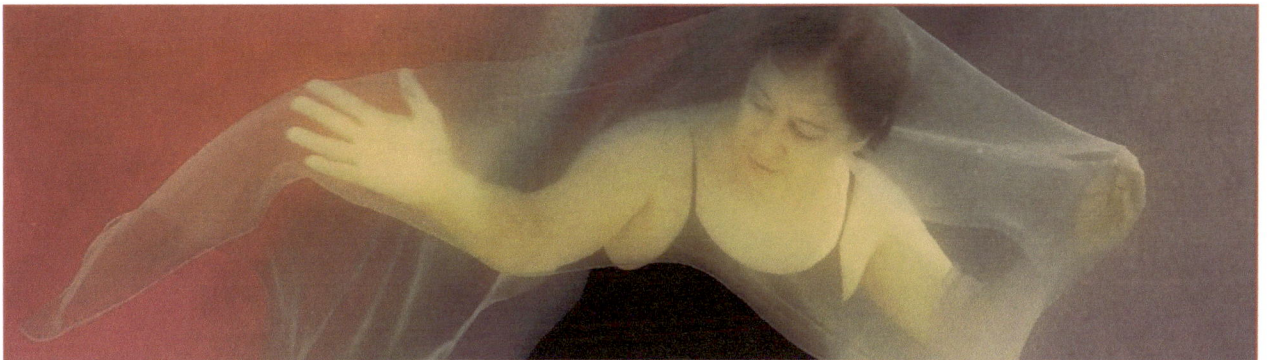

Photo Chris Graefe

Ruth Lieberherr is a writer, artist and illustrator. She has written and illustrated the picturebooks *The Caterpillar and the Butterfly (Die Raupe und der Schmetterling)* and *The Boy Without A Name (Der Bub Ohne Namen)*. She illustrated the following picturebooks: *By Some Great Spell* (author Mary Beth Melton), *Hafez, The Mathematical Stonecutter* (author Michael Punzak), *The Knottles* (author Nancy Mellon), *Journey to Inner Space* (author Deborah R. Cohen) and *Winter, Awake!* (author Linda Kroll).

Lieberherr's award-winning paintings have been exhibited in solo and group exhibits in galleries and cultural centers in the United States, Switzerland and France. Originally from Switzerland, Lieberherr lives with her husband outside of Boston in Massachusetts, USA. She is the mother of two daughters and grandmother of four grandchildren. She is also a yoga teacher and dancer.

www.RuthLieberherr.com

www.ingramcontent.com/pod-product-compliance
Lightning Source LLC
Chambersburg PA
CBHW041154070526
44584CB00004B/309